WHAT IS A SECRET CODE?

SHINOY AND THE CHAOS CREW

Contents

Written by Stevie Derrick

Collins

What are secret codes?

People have been writing secret messages for
thousands of years. These messages were hidden,
using ways of writing called codes. A code is like
a puzzle where letters of the alphabet are swapped
with other letters, numbers or pictures.

To understand the message,
you need a **key** that tells
you what letters have been
swapped and how to put
them back in order.

Why do people use codes?

People use codes to keep secret information hidden. A spy is a person whose job is to find out secrets about another country. Spies use codes to hide messages from their enemies.

a secret hiding place in a shoe

a secret code hidden in a walnut

Codes can also keep information about your life secret. Over 350 years ago, a man called Samuel Pepys wrote a diary in code so people couldn't read it. At the time, Pepys worked for King Charles II. In his diary, he called King Charles "silly" for playing with his dogs too much, and the king couldn't read it!

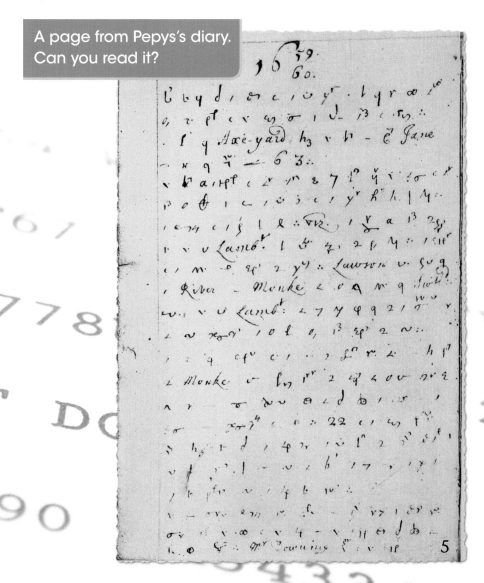

A page from Pepys's diary. Can you read it?

Codes aren't always secret. In fact, codes are all around you. You might use codes when playing sports – teams use different colours to show who's on which side. Your teacher might use a code, like holding up their hand, when they want the class to be quiet. Codes are useful in everyday life because they allow information to be told quickly.

These footballers are on the same team.

A green man means you can cross the road.

Who created the first code?

One of the first codes was discovered in the **tomb** of an ancient Egyptian man called Khnumhotep II. Inside it, is the story of Khnumhotep's life written in an ancient form of writing called hieroglyphics. However, some of the hieroglyphics in Khnumhotep's tomb were swapped with other pictures that people didn't know.

Hieroglyphics use pictures instead of words.

7

What is Morse code?

Morse code is one of the most famous codes in history, but it's not a secret code. Samuel Morse invented it in 1838, and his code allowed information to be sent quickly in a way that everyone could understand. The code swapped letters in the alphabet for a pattern of dots and dashes.

The message was tapped out by an operator on an electronic device, called a telegraph key, using short and long sounds. The message could be sent hundreds of kilometres through wires, and an operator on the other end would listen to the message and **decode** it.

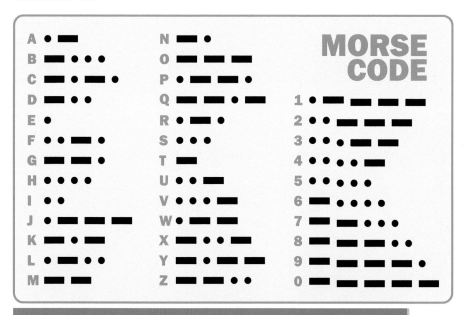

All the operators had the same Morse code book.

Sending a message by telegraph was quicker than sending a letter.

9

Are any other codes used for sending messages?

Smoke signals are one of the oldest forms of sending messages over a long distance. They were first used more than 2,000 years ago to send information along the Great Wall of China. One puff of smoke meant attention, two puffs meant everything was OK, while three puffs signalled danger.

Semaphore is another type of communication but it uses flags, not smoke. It was used during the 19th century as a way of sending messages between ships. A person on one ship would hold a small flag in each hand with their arms held out. They positioned their arms at different angles and each movement represented a letter of the alphabet or number.

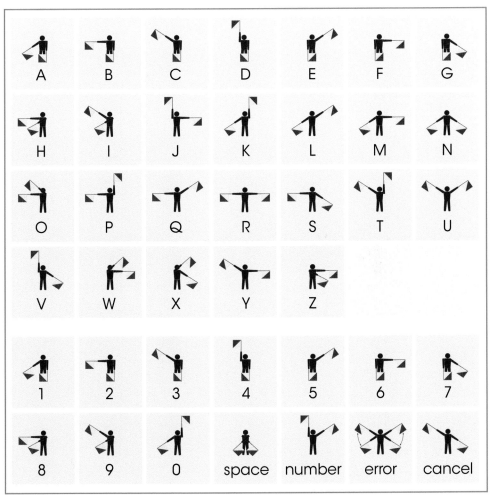

When are secret codes used the most?

Secret codes are used during wartime to stop information from falling into the wrong hands. During the First and Second World War, codes that worked by swapping military words for words that didn't mean anything were used to hide secrets. For example, "captain" was swapped for "lower". This is a substitution code.

Code word L	Code No 490	Message or true reading.
Loved	00	Merciful
Loveful	01	Mercifully
Loveless	02	Merciless
Lovelier	03	Mercilessly
Loveliest	04	Mercy
Lovelily	05	At the mercy of
Loveliness	06	Mere
Lovelock	07	Merely
Lovelorn	08	And it merely
Lovely	09	Are merely
Lovemaking	10	Are merely the
Lovemonger	11	Is merely
Lover	12	Is not merely
Lovers	13	It merely
Loverwise	14	Not merely
Loves	15	Was merely
Lovesick	16	Were merely
Lovesome	17	Were not merely
Loving	18	Will be merely
Lovingly	19	Will merely
Lovingness	20	Merest
Lowbell	21	Merge
Lowborn	22	To merge
Lowbred	23	Merged
Lowchurch	24	Merges
Lowed	25	Merging
Lowell	26	Merida
Lower	27	Meridian
Lowercase	28	Ante-meridian (A. M.)
Lowered	29	Post-meridian (P. M.)
Lowering	30	Merit
Loweringly	31	Does it merit serious consideration
Lowermost	32	Does merit serious consideration
Lowers	33	Does not merit serious consideration
Lowery	34	Merited
Lowest	35	Not merited
Lowing	36	Well merited
Lowings	37	Meriting
Lowish	38	Meritorious
Lowland	39	Meritoriously
Lowlander	40	Merits
Lowlanders	41	Mersine
Lowlier	42	Meshed
Lowliest	43	Meshes
Lowlihead	44	Mess
Lowlihood	45	Message
Lowlily	46	A message
Lowliness	47	A message from
Lowlived	48	No message from
Lowly	49	The message

Code word L	Code No 490	Message or true reading.
		Message—Continued
	50	The message of
Lowminded	51	The message will be
Lownecked	52	Messages
Lowness	53	Messenger
Lowry	54	By messenger
Lowstudded	55	Has messenger arrived
Loyal	56	Has messenger left
Loyalist	57	Have sent a messenger
Loyalists	58	Messenger has arrived
Loyally	59	Messenger has left
Loyalness	60	Messenger has not arrived
Loyalty	61	Your messenger has arrived
Lozenge	62	Your messenger has not arrived
Lozenged	63	Your messenger left
Lozenges	64	Messengers
Lozengy	65	Messieurs
Lubbard	66	Messina
Lubber	67	Messrs.
Lubberly	68	Met
Lubbers	69	Met by
Lubec	70	Met with
Lubric	71	Metal
Lubrical	72	Metallic
Lubricant	73	Metals
Lubricants	74	Metaphor
Lubricate	75	Metaphoric
Lubricated	76	Metaphorical
Lubricates	77	Metaphorically
Lubricator	78	Metaphors
Lubricity	79	Mete
Lubricous	80	Meted
Luce	81	Meteorological
Lucency	82	Meter
Lucent	83	Meters
Lucern	84	Metes
Lucernal	85	Method
Lucid	86	By this method
Lucidity	87	By what method
Lucidly	88	Method of
Lucidness	89	The method
Lucifer	90	Methodical
Luciferian	91	Methodically
Luciferous	92	Methodist
Lucifers	93	Methodists
Lucific	94	Methodize
Luciform	95	Methodized
Lucifrian	96	Methodizes
Luctmeter	97	Methodizing
Lucimeters	98	Methods
Luck	99	Metric
Luckier		

Individual letters can also be substituted. The top line shows the alphabet; the bottom line shows the alphabet written backwards. Using this simple code, "The soldiers will march in the morning" becomes "Gsv hlowrvih droo nzixs rm gsv nlimrmt".

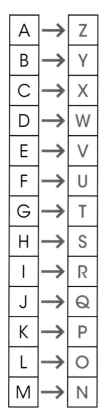
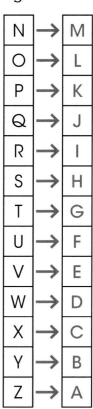

The letters could be written in any order on the second line. A codebook showing what words or letters had been swapped allowed people to decode the messages.

In 1918, the US army came up with the idea of using the language spoken by Choctaw Native American soldiers to pass important information to each other over the telephone, which was then relayed in English to the other soldiers. Only a handful of people knew the language, so this code was almost impossible for anyone else to understand. During the Second World War, Navajo Native American soldiers passed messages in the same way.

Navajo soldiers, 1943

Did you know?
The Choctaw language didn't have words for some of the military terms, so they created different words. For example, a group of soldiers was a "tribe".

How were messages delivered?

Soldiers used other ways to send secret information quickly. Pigeons flew to soldiers in the **trenches** during battles to warn of an attack. They carried messages in small tubes attached to their legs.

Messenger dogs were quick and able to run through battlefields more easily than people. They carried messages between the trenches, took medicine to wounded soldiers and sniffed out the enemy.

Are there coding machines?

The Enigma machine was a coding machine invented after the First World War by a German man named Arthur Scherbius. It looked like a large typewriter and had a different key for every letter in the alphabet.

When a person typed a message, the machine would scramble it, so it didn't appear to make any sense. To unscramble the message, people needed to have an identical machine with the same settings.

Did you know?
The word "enigma" means something mysterious or difficult to understand.

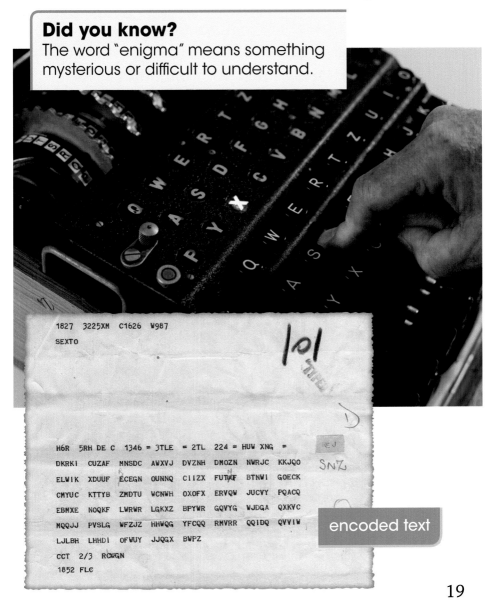

encoded text

How was the Enigma machine used?

The Enigma machine was used by Germany to send secret messages during the Second World War.

Germany thought its Enigma machine was impossible to work out because there were so many ways a message could be coded. The chances of breaking the codes were around 158 million million million – that's 158 with 18 zeros – to one.

German soldiers using an Enigma machine

What is a codebreaker?

The science of writing and solving codes is called cryptography. Cryptologists – also known as codebreakers – use maths to solve codes by finding patterns in them.

Is there a school for codebreakers?

Yes! Bletchley Park in Milton Keynes, UK, was home to the Government Code and Cipher School. It opened in 1939 and was like a secret hideout for codebreakers.

Codebreakers built a machine called the Bombe that could work out the messages.

Bletchley Park codebreakers, 1942–43

the Bombe machine

23

Who were the best codebreakers?

The codebreakers of Bletchley Park played an important part in winning the war. Two of the most famous codebreakers were Alan Turing and Joan Clarke. They, and other codebreakers, shortened the war by two years and saved millions of lives.

Alan Turing

Joan Clarke

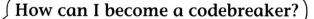
How can I become a codebreaker?

Are you good at maths? Do you like solving puzzles like crosswords? If you do, you might have the right skills to become a codebreaker! Today, codebreakers usually need a university degree in maths or computer science.

Are there any unbreakable codes?

More than 200 years ago, a man named
Thomas Beale wrote three coded messages. He said
that anyone who solved the messages would find
a **hoard** of incredible treasure. The messages were
written using simple substitution codes where numbers
represent a letter of the alphabet.

However, the keys to the codes are unknown texts.
By chance, a codebreaker in the 19th century worked
out one code, but no one has ever found the keys to
the other codes, or the missing treasure ... yet.

Glossary

decode work out the meaning of a coded message

hoard a collection of valuable objects

key something that tells you how to unscramble a code

tomb a large room, sometimes underground, where people bury the dead

trenches long, narrow ditches where soldiers would live and fight during the war

Index

Make codes work for you!

Substitution code

	A	D	F	G	V	X
A	C	O	9	X	F	4
D	M	K	3	A	Z	9
F	N	W	L	0	J	D
G	5	S	I	Y	H	U
V	P	1	V	B	6	R
X	E	Q	7	T	2	G

GV	XA	FF	FF	AD
H	E	L	L	O

Morse code

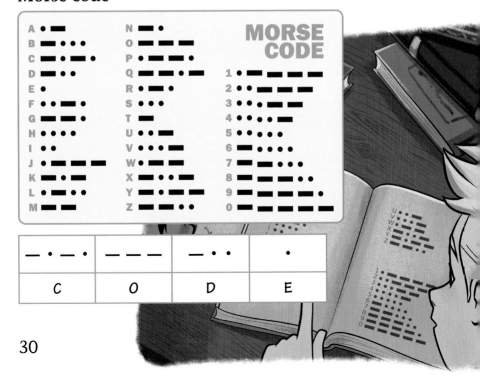

— · — ·	— — —	— · ·	·
C	O	D	E

Semaphore

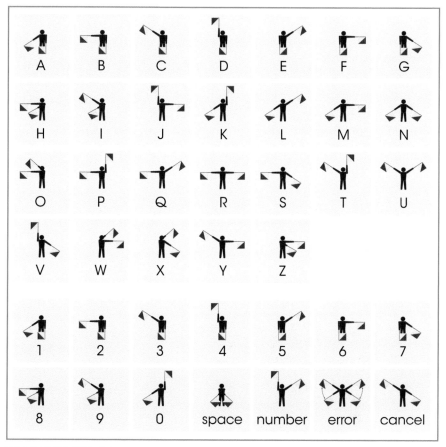

Grab a pen and paper and use these codes to write your own secret messages.

Ideas for reading

Written by Christine Whitney

Primary Literacy Consultant

Reading objectives:
- retrieve information from non-fiction
- be introduced to non-fiction books that are structured in different ways
- explain and discuss their understanding of books

Spoken language objectives:
- ask relevant questions
- speculate, imagine and explore ideas through talk
- participate in discussions

Curriculum links: History: Develop an awareness of the past; Writing: Write for different purposes

Word count: 1327

Interest words: codes, codebreaker, decode, hieroglyphics, semaphore

Resources: lemon, water, bowl, cotton buds, white paper, materials for making flags

Build a context for reading

- Ask children what they understand by the phrase *secret code*. Who do they think would use a secret code?
- Read the title of the book and encourage children to ask three questions about secret codes.
- As a group, make a list of all the ways messages can be sent nowadays.

Understand and apply reading strategies

- Read up to page 6 together and ask children to find one example of when codes might be secret and one example of when codes are not secret.
- Continue to read to page 11. Ask children to identify the different types of codes used for sending messages.
- How were messages delivered in the past? Ask children to find the page where the answer to this question will be found.
- Continue to read to page 25 and then discuss as a group what they know about *codebreakers*.
- Look closely at the index. What does it tell the reader? How is this different from the contents page?